199

GERMAN SHEPHERDS

WEEKLY ENGAGEMENT CALENDAR
FEATURING 53 FULL-COLOR IMAGES

THANKS TO YOU, OUR CUSTOMERS, BrownTrout is pleased to offer an expanded line of calendars for 1998 with over 500 titles on a variety of subjects from wilderness and national parks to castles, poets, plants, wildlife, cats, dogs and dog breeds, horses, lighthouses, rural America, sports, Canada, Mexico, travel, U.S. cities, and American states.

If you are interested in other calendars or books published by BrownTrout, please ask your local bookstore to special order them for you. Your bookseller can search for a complete list of our titles under the BrownTrout ISBN prefix: 0-7631-0.

For further assistance in finding a particular title, visit our website:

http://www.browntrout.com
or fax: 310 316 1138
or telephone: 800 777 7812

A note about our calendars:
All moon phases, seasons, and holidays are designated in Universal Time (U.T.), which is the same as Greenwich Mean Time. Therefore, the reader should subtract five hours for the equivalent time on the East Coast of the United States, which in some cases may change the dates of certain events.

BROWNTROUT PUBLISHERS, INC.
POST OFFICE BOX 280070
SAN FRANCISCO, CALIFORNIA 94128-0070

DECEMBER 1997

S	M	T	W	T	F	S
	1	2	3	4	5	6
7	8	9	10	11	12	13
14	15	16	17	18	19	20
21	22	23	24	25	26	27
28	29	30	31			

DEC. 1997 - JAN. 1998

Sunday,
DECEMBER
28

Monday,
DECEMBER
29

Tuesday,
DECEMBER
30

Wednesday,
DECEMBER
31
New Year's Eve

Thursday,
JANUARY
1
New Year's Day

JANUARY 1998

S	M	T	W	T	F	S
				1	2	3
4	5	6	7	8	9	10
11	12	13	14	15	16	17
18	19	20	21	22	23	24
25	26	27	28	29	30	31

Friday,
JANUARY
2

Saturday,
JANUARY
3

JANUARY 1998

JANUARY

S	M	T	W	T	F	S
				1	2	3
4	5	6	7	8	9	10
11	12	13	14	15	16	17
18	19	20	21	22	23	24
25	26	27	28	29	30	31

Sunday,
JANUARY
4

Monday,
JANUARY
5

Tuesday,
JANUARY
6

Wednesday,
JANUARY
7

Thursday,
JANUARY
8

Friday,
JANUARY
9

Saturday,
JANUARY
10

JANUARY

S	M	T	W	T	F	S
				1	2	3
4	5	6	7	8	9	10
11	12	13	14	15	16	17
18	19	20	21	22	23	24
25	26	27	28	29	30	31

JANUARY 1998

Sunday,
JANUARY
11

Monday,
JANUARY
12
Full Moon

Tuesday,
JANUARY
13

Wednesday,
JANUARY
14

Thursday,
JANUARY
15

Friday,
JANUARY
16

Saturday,
JANUARY
17

JANUARY 1998

JANUARY

S	M	T	W	T	F	S
				1	2	3
4	5	6	7	8	9	10
11	12	13	14	15	16	17
18	19	20	21	22	23	24
25	26	27	28	29	30	31

Sunday,
JANUARY
18

Monday,
JANUARY
19
Martin Luther King, Jr.
Birthday (Observed)

Tuesday,
JANUARY
20

Wednesday,
JANUARY
21

Thursday,
JANUARY
22

Friday,
JANUARY
23

Saturday,
JANUARY
24

JANUARY

S	M	T	W	T	F	S
				1	2	3
4	5	6	7	8	9	10
11	12	13	14	15	16	17
18	19	20	21	22	23	24
25	26	27	28	29	30	31

JANUARY 1998

Sunday,
JANUARY
25

Monday,
JANUARY
26
Australia Day

Tuesday,
JANUARY
27

Wednesday,
JANUARY
28
New Moon

Thursday,
JANUARY
29

Friday,
JANUARY
30

Saturday,
JANUARY
31

FEBRUARY 1998

FEBRUARY

S	M	T	W	T	F	S
1	2	3	4	5	6	7
8	9	10	11	12	13	14
15	16	17	18	19	20	21
22	23	24	25	26	27	28

Sunday,
FEBRUARY
1

Monday,
FEBRUARY
2
Groundhog Day

Tuesday,
FEBRUARY
3

Wednesday,
FEBRUARY
4

Thursday,
FEBRUARY
5

Friday,
FEBRUARY
6

Saturday,
FEBRUARY
7

FEBRUARY

S	M	T	W	T	F	S
1	2	3	4	5	6	7
8	9	10	11	12	13	14
15	16	17	18	19	20	21
22	23	24	25	26	27	28

FEBRUARY 1998

Sunday,
FEBRUARY
8

Monday,
FEBRUARY
9

Tuesday,
FEBRUARY
10

Wednesday,
FEBRUARY
11
Full Moon

Thursday,
FEBRUARY
12
Abraham Lincoln's Birthday

Friday,
FEBRUARY
13

Saturday,
FEBRUARY
14
St. Valentine's Day

©1997 FAITH A. URIDEL

FEBRUARY 1998

FEBRUARY

S	M	T	W	T	F	S
1	2	3	4	5	6	7
8	9	10	11	12	13	14
15	16	17	18	19	20	21
22	23	24	25	26	27	28

Sunday,
FEBRUARY
15

Monday,
FEBRUARY
16
George Washington's
Birthday (Observed)
Presidents' Day

Tuesday,
FEBRUARY
17

Wednesday,
FEBRUARY
18

Thursday,
FEBRUARY
19

Friday,
FEBRUARY
20

Saturday,
FEBRUARY
21

FEBRUARY

S	M	T	W	T	F	S
1	2	3	4	5	6	7
8	9	10	11	12	13	14
15	16	17	18	19	20	21
22	23	24	25	26	27	28

FEBRUARY 1998

Sunday,
FEBRUARY
22
George Washington's Birthday

Monday,
FEBRUARY
23

Tuesday,
FEBRUARY
24
Mardi Gras

Wednesday,
FEBRUARY
25
Ash Wednesday

Thursday,
FEBRUARY
26
New Moon
Total Solar Eclipse
(Path: from Mongolia across
Siberia, almost to North Pole)

Friday,
FEBRUARY
27

Saturday,
FEBRUARY
28

		MARCH				
S	M	T	W	T	F	S
1	2	3	4	5	6	7
8	9	10	11	12	13	14
15	16	17	18	19	20	21
22	23	24	25	26	27	28
29	30	31				

MARCH 1998

Sunday,
MARCH
1

Monday,
MARCH
2

Tuesday,
MARCH
3

Wednesday,
MARCH
4

Thursday,
MARCH
5

Friday,
MARCH
6

Saturday,
MARCH
7

MARCH

S	M	T	W	T	F	S
1	2	3	4	5	6	7
8	9	10	11	12	13	14
15	16	17	18	19	20	21
22	23	24	25	26	27	28
29	30	31				

MARCH 1998

Sunday,
MARCH
8

Monday,
MARCH
9

Tuesday,
MARCH
10

Wednesday,
MARCH
11

Thursday,
MARCH
12
Full Moon
Purim (Feast of Lots)

Friday,
MARCH
13

Saturday,
MARCH
14

MARCH 1998

MARCH

S	M	T	W	T	F	S
1	2	3	4	5	6	7
8	9	10	11	12	13	14
15	16	17	18	19	20	21
22	23	24	25	26	27	28
29	30	31				

Sunday,
MARCH
15

Monday,
MARCH
16

Tuesday,
MARCH
17
St. Patrick's Day

Wednesday,
MARCH
18

Thursday,
MARCH
19

Friday,
MARCH
20
Vernal Equinox

Saturday,
MARCH
21

MARCH

S	M	T	W	T	F	S
1	2	3	4	5	6	7
8	9	10	11	12	13	14
15	16	17	18	19	20	21
22	23	24	25	26	27	28
29	30	31				

MARCH 1998

Sunday,
MARCH
22
Mother's Day (U.K.)

Monday,
MARCH
23

Tuesday,
MARCH
24

Wednesday,
MARCH
25

Thursday,
MARCH
26

Friday,
MARCH
27

Saturday,
MARCH
28
New Moon

MARCH-APRIL 1998

MARCH

S	M	T	W	T	F	S
1	2	3	4	5	6	7
8	9	10	11	12	13	14
15	16	17	18	19	20	21
22	23	24	25	26	27	28
29	30	31				

Sunday,
MARCH
29

Monday,
MARCH
30

Tuesday,
MARCH
31

APRIL

S	M	T	W	T	F	S
			1	2	3	4
5	6	7	8	9	10	11
12	13	14	15	16	17	18
19	20	21	22	23	24	25
26	27	28	29	30		

Wednesday,
APRIL
1
April Fool's Day

Thursday,
APRIL
2

Friday,
APRIL
3

Saturday,
APRIL
4

APRIL

S	M	T	W	T	F	S
			1	2	3	4
5	6	7	8	9	10	11
12	13	14	15	16	17	18
19	20	21	22	23	24	25
26	27	28	29	30		

APRIL 1998

Sunday,
APRIL
5
Daylight Savings Begins
(U.S.)

Monday,
APRIL
6

Tuesday,
APRIL
7

Wednesday,
APRIL
8

Thursday,
APRIL
9

Friday,
APRIL
10
Good Friday

Saturday,
APRIL
11
Full Moon
Pesach (Passover)

APRIL 1998

APRIL

S	M	T	W	T	F	S
			1	2	3	4
5	6	7	8	9	10	11
12	13	14	15	16	17	18
19	20	21	22	23	24	25
26	27	28	29	30		

Sunday,
APRIL
12
Easter Sunday

Monday,
APRIL
13
Easter Monday

Tuesday,
APRIL
14

Wednesday,
APRIL
15

Thursday,
APRIL
16

Friday,
APRIL
17

Saturday,
APRIL
18

APRIL

S	M	T	W	T	F	S
			1	2	3	4
5	6	7	8	9	10	11
12	13	14	15	16	17	18
19	20	21	22	23	24	25
26	27	28	29	30		

APRIL 1998

Sunday,
APRIL
19

Monday,
APRIL
20

Tuesday,
APRIL
21

Wednesday,
APRIL
22
Earth Day

Thursday,
APRIL
23

Friday,
APRIL
24
Arbor Day

Saturday,
APRIL
25
ANZAC Day (Australia)

APRIL-MAY 1998

APRIL

S	M	T	W	T	F	S
			1	2	3	4
5	6	7	8	9	10	11
12	13	14	15	16	17	18
19	20	21	22	23	24	25
26	27	28	29	30		

Sunday,
APRIL
26
New Moon

Monday,
APRIL
27

Tuesday,
APRIL
28

Wednesday,
APRIL
29

Thursday,
APRIL
30

MAY

S	M	T	W	T	F	S
					1	2
3	4	5	6	7	8	9
10	11	12	13	14	15	16
17	18	19	20	21	22	23
24	25	26	27	28	29	30
31						

Friday,
MAY
1
May Day

Saturday,
MAY
2

		MAY				
S	M	T	W	T	F	S
					1	2
3	4	5	6	7	8	9
10	11	12	13	14	15	16
17	18	19	20	21	22	23
24	25	26	27	28	29	30
31						

MAY 1998

Sunday,
MAY
3

Monday,
MAY
4
Holiday (U.K.)

Tuesday,
MAY
5
Cinco de Mayo

Wednesday,
MAY
6

Thursday,
MAY
7

Friday,
MAY
8

Saturday,
MAY
9

MAY

S	M	T	W	T	F	S
					1	2
3	4	5	6	7	8	9
10	11	12	13	14	15	16
17	18	19	20	21	22	23
24	25	26	27	28	29	30
31						

MAY 1998

Sunday,
MAY
10
Mother's Day (U.S.)

Monday,
MAY
11
Full Moon

Tuesday,
MAY
12

Wednesday,
MAY
13

Thursday,
MAY
14

Friday,
MAY
15

Saturday,
MAY
16

MAY

S	M	T	W	T	F	S
					1	2
3	4	5	6	7	8	9
10	11	12	13	14	15	16
17	18	19	20	21	22	23
24	25	26	27	28	29	30
31						

MAY 1998

Sunday,
MAY
17

Monday,
MAY
18
Victoria Day (Canada)

Tuesday,
MAY
19

Wednesday,
MAY
20

Thursday,
MAY
21

Friday,
MAY
22

Saturday,
MAY
23

MAY 1998

MAY

S	M	T	W	T	F	S
					1	2
3	4	5	6	7	8	9
10	11	12	13	14	15	16
17	18	19	20	21	22	23
24	25	26	27	28	29	30
31						

Sunday,
MAY
24

Monday,
MAY
25
New Moon
Memorial Day (Observed)
Holiday (U.K.)

Tuesday,
MAY
26

Wednesday,
MAY
27

Thursday,
MAY
28

Friday,
MAY
29

Saturday,
MAY
30

MAY

S	M	T	W	T	F	S
					1	2
3	4	5	6	7	8	9
10	11	12	13	14	15	16
17	18	19	20	21	22	23
24	25	26	27	28	29	30
31						

MAY-JUNE 1998

Sunday,
MAY
31
Pentecost
Shavuoth (Feast of Weeks)

Monday,
JUNE
1

JUNE

S	M	T	W	T	F	S
	1	2	3	4	5	6
7	8	9	10	11	12	13
14	15	16	17	18	19	20
21	22	23	24	25	26	27
28	29	30				

Tuesday,
JUNE
2

Wednesday,
JUNE
3

Thursday,
JUNE
4

Friday,
JUNE
5

Saturday,
JUNE
6

©1997 ELIZABETH FLYNN

JUNE 1998

JUNE

S	M	T	W	T	F	S
	1	2	3	4	5	6
7	8	9	10	11	12	13
14	15	16	17	18	19	20
21	22	23	24	25	26	27
28	29	30				

Sunday,
JUNE
7

Monday,
JUNE
8

Tuesday,
JUNE
9

Wednesday,
JUNE
10
Full Moon

Thursday,
JUNE
11

Friday,
JUNE
12

Saturday,
JUNE
13

JUNE

S	M	T	W	T	F	S
	1	2	3	4	5	6
7	8	9	10	11	12	13
14	15	16	17	18	19	20
21	22	23	24	25	26	27
28	29	30				

JUNE 1998

Sunday,
JUNE
14

Monday,
JUNE
15

Tuesday,
JUNE
16

Wednesday,
JUNE
17

Thursday,
JUNE
18

Friday,
JUNE
19

Saturday,
JUNE
20

J U N E

S	M	T	W	T	F	S
	1	2	3	4	5	6
7	8	9	10	11	12	13
14	15	16	17	18	19	20
21	22	23	24	25	26	27
28	29	30				

JUNE 1998

Sunday,
JUNE
21
Father's Day
Summer Solstice

Monday,
JUNE
22

Tuesday,
JUNE
23

Wednesday,
JUNE
24
New Moon
St.-Jean Baptiste Day (Quebec)

Thursday,
JUNE
25

Friday,
JUNE
26

Saturday,
JUNE
27

JUNE

S	M	T	W	T	F	S
	1	2	3	4	5	6
7	8	9	10	11	12	13
14	15	16	17	18	19	20
21	22	23	24	25	26	27
28	29	30				

JUNE-JULY 1998

Sunday,
JUNE
28

Monday,
JUNE
29

Tuesday,
JUNE
30

Wednesday,
JULY
1
Canada Day

JULY

S	M	T	W	T	F	S
			1	2	3	4
5	6	7	8	9	10	11
12	13	14	15	16	17	18
19	20	21	22	23	24	25
26	27	28	29	30	31	

Thursday,
JULY
2

Friday,
JULY
3

Saturday,
JULY
4
Independence Day

©1997 PAULETTE BRAUN

JULY 1998

J U L Y

S	M	T	W	T	F	S
			1	2	3	4
5	6	7	8	9	10	11
12	13	14	15	16	17	18
19	20	21	22	23	24	25
26	27	28	29	30	31	

Sunday,
JULY
5

Monday,
JULY
6

Tuesday,
JULY
7

Wednesday,
JULY
8

Thursday,
JULY
9
Full Moon

Friday,
JULY
10

Saturday,
JULY
11

JULY

S	M	T	W	T	F	S
			1	2	3	4
5	6	7	8	9	10	11
12	13	14	15	16	17	18
19	20	21	22	23	24	25
26	27	28	29	30	31	

JULY 1998

Sunday,
JULY
12

Monday,
JULY
13

Tuesday,
JULY
14
Bastille Day (France)

Wednesday,
JULY
15

Thursday,
JULY
16

Friday,
JULY
17

Saturday,
JULY
18

©1997 MARK RAYCROFT

JULY 1998

JULY

S	M	T	W	T	F	S
			1	2	3	4
5	6	7	8	9	10	11
12	13	14	15	16	17	18
19	20	21	22	23	24	25
26	27	28	29	30	31	

Sunday,
JULY
19

Monday,
JULY
20

Tuesday,
JULY
21

Wednesday,
JULY
22

Thursday,
JULY
23
New Moon

Friday,
JULY
24

Saturday,
JULY
25

JULY

S	M	T	W	T	F	S
			1	2	3	4
5	6	7	8	9	10	11
12	13	14	15	16	17	18
19	20	21	22	23	24	25
26	27	28	29	30	31	

JULY-AUGUST 1998

Sunday,
JULY
26

Monday,
JULY
27

Tuesday,
JULY
28

Wednesday,
JULY
29

Thursday,
JULY
30

Friday,
JULY
31

Saturday,
AUGUST
1

AUGUST

S	M	T	W	T	F	S
						1
2	3	4	5	6	7	8
9	10	11	12	13	14	15
16	17	18	19	20	21	22
23	24	25	26	27	28	29
30	31					

©1997 MARK RAYCROFT

AUGUST 1998

AUGUST

S	M	T	W	T	F	S
						1
2	3	4	5	6	7	8
9	10	11	12	13	14	15
16	17	18	19	20	21	22
23	24	25	26	27	28	29
30	31					

Sunday,
AUGUST
2

Monday,
AUGUST
3

Tuesday,
AUGUST
4

Wednesday,
AUGUST
5

Thursday,
AUGUST
6

Friday,
AUGUST
7

Saturday,
AUGUST
8
Full Moon

AUGUST

S	M	T	W	T	F	S
						1
2	3	4	5	6	7	8
9	10	11	12	13	14	15
16	17	18	19	20	21	22
23	24	25	26	27	28	29
30	31					

AUGUST 1998

Sunday,
AUGUST
9

Monday,
AUGUST
10

Tuesday,
AUGUST
11

Wednesday,
AUGUST
12

Thursday,
AUGUST
13

Friday,
AUGUST
14

Saturday,
AUGUST
15

AUGUST

S	M	T	W	T	F	S
						1
2	3	4	5	6	7	8
9	10	11	12	13	14	15
16	17	18	19	20	21	22
23	24	25	26	27	28	29
30	31					

AUGUST 1998

Sunday,
AUGUST
16

Monday,
AUGUST
17

Tuesday,
AUGUST
18

Wednesday,
AUGUST
19

Thursday,
AUGUST
20

Friday,
AUGUST
21

Saturday,
AUGUST
22
New Moon

AUGUST

S	M	T	W	T	F	S
						1
2	3	4	5	6	7	8
9	10	11	12	13	14	15
16	17	18	19	20	21	22
23	24	25	26	27	28	29
30	31					

AUGUST 1998

Sunday,
AUGUST
23

Monday,
AUGUST
24

Tuesday,
AUGUST
25

Wednesday,
AUGUST
26

Thursday,
AUGUST
27

Friday,
AUGUST
28

Saturday,
AUGUST
29

AUG.-SEPT. 1998

AUGUST

S	M	T	W	T	F	S
						1
2	3	4	5	6	7	8
9	10	11	12	13	14	15
16	17	18	19	20	21	22
23	24	25	26	27	28	29
30	31					

Sunday,
AUGUST
30

Monday,
AUGUST
31
Holiday (U.K.)

SEPTEMBER

S	M	T	W	T	F	S
		1	2	3	4	5
6	7	8	9	10	11	12
13	14	15	16	17	18	19
20	21	22	23	24	25	26
27	28	29	30			

Tuesday,
SEPTEMBER
1

Wednesday,
SEPTEMBER
2

Thursday,
SEPTEMBER
3

Friday,
SEPTEMBER
4

Saturday,
SEPTEMBER
5

SEPTEMBER

S	M	T	W	T	F	S
		1	2	3	4	5
6	7	8	9	10	11	12
13	14	15	16	17	18	19
20	21	22	23	24	25	26
27	28	29	30			

SEPTEMBER 1998

Sunday,
SEPTEMBER
6
Full Moon

Monday,
SEPTEMBER
7
Labor Day

Tuesday,
SEPTEMBER
8

Wednesday,
SEPTEMBER
9

Thursday,
SEPTEMBER
10

Friday,
SEPTEMBER
11

Saturday,
SEPTEMBER
12

SEPTEMBER

S	M	T	W	T	F	S
		1	2	3	4	5
6	7	8	9	10	11	12
13	14	15	16	17	18	19
20	21	22	23	24	25	26
27	28	29	30			

SEPTEMBER 1998

Sunday,
SEPTEMBER
13

Monday,
SEPTEMBER
14

Tuesday,
SEPTEMBER
15

Wednesday,
SEPTEMBER
16
Independence Day (Mexico)

Thursday,
SEPTEMBER
17

Friday,
SEPTEMBER
18

Saturday,
SEPTEMBER
19

SEPTEMBER

S	M	T	W	T	F	S
		1	2	3	4	5
6	7	8	9	10	11	12
13	14	15	16	17	18	19
20	21	22	23	24	25	26
27	28	29	30			

SEPTEMBER 1998

Sunday,
SEPTEMBER
20
New Moon

Monday,
SEPTEMBER
21
Rosh Hashanah (New Year)

Tuesday,
SEPTEMBER
22

Wednesday,
SEPTEMBER
23
Autumnal Equinox

Thursday,
SEPTEMBER
24

Friday,
SEPTEMBER
25

Saturday,
SEPTEMBER
26

©1997 MARK RAYCROFT

SEPTEMBER

S	M	T	W	T	F	S
		1	2	3	4	5
6	7	8	9	10	11	12
13	14	15	16	17	18	19
20	21	22	23	24	25	26
27	28	29	30			

SEPT.-OCT. 1998

Sunday,
SEPTEMBER
27

Monday,
SEPTEMBER
28

Tuesday,
SEPTEMBER
29

Wednesday,
SEPTEMBER
30
Yom Kippur
(Day of Atonement)

OCTOBER

S	M	T	W	T	F	S
				1	2	3
4	5	6	7	8	9	10
11	12	13	14	15	16	17
18	19	20	21	22	23	24
25	26	27	28	29	30	31

Thursday,
OCTOBER
1

Friday,
OCTOBER
2

Saturday,
OCTOBER
3

OCTOBER

S	M	T	W	T	F	S
				1	2	3
4	5	6	7	8	9	10
11	12	13	14	15	16	17
18	19	20	21	22	23	24
25	26	27	28	29	30	31

OCTOBER 1998

Sunday,
OCTOBER
4

Monday,
OCTOBER
5
Full Moon
Sukkoth (Tabernacles)

Tuesday,
OCTOBER
6

Wednesday,
OCTOBER
7

Thursday,
OCTOBER
8

Friday,
OCTOBER
9

Saturday,
OCTOBER
10

©1997 SHARON EIDE

OCTOBER 1998

OCTOBER

S	M	T	W	T	F	S
				1	2	3
4	5	6	7	8	9	10
11	12	13	14	15	16	17
18	19	20	21	22	23	24
25	26	27	28	29	30	31

Sunday,
OCTOBER
11

Monday,
OCTOBER
12
Columbus Day
Thanksgiving Day (Canada)

Tuesday,
OCTOBER
13

Wednesday,
OCTOBER
14

Thursday,
OCTOBER
15

Friday,
OCTOBER
16

Saturday,
OCTOBER
17

OCTOBER

S	M	T	W	T	F	S
				1	2	3
4	5	6	7	8	9	10
11	12	13	14	15	16	17
18	19	20	21	22	23	24
25	26	27	28	29	30	31

OCTOBER 1998

Sunday,
OCTOBER
18

Monday,
OCTOBER
19

Tuesday,
OCTOBER
20
New Moon

Wednesday,
OCTOBER
21

Thursday,
OCTOBER
22

Friday,
OCTOBER
23

Saturday,
OCTOBER
24
United Nations Day

©1997 MARK RAYCROFT

OCTOBER

S	M	T	W	T	F	S
				1	2	3
4	5	6	7	8	9	10
11	12	13	14	15	16	17
18	19	20	21	22	23	24
25	26	27	28	29	30	31

OCTOBER 1998

Sunday,
OCTOBER
25
Daylight Savings Ends
(U.S.)

Monday,
OCTOBER
26

Tuesday,
OCTOBER
27

Wednesday,
OCTOBER
28

Thursday,
OCTOBER
29

Friday,
OCTOBER
30

Saturday,
OCTOBER
31
Halloween

NOVEMBER

S	M	T	W	T	F	S
1	2	3	4	5	6	7
8	9	10	11	12	13	14
15	16	17	18	19	20	21
22	23	24	25	26	27	28
29	30					

NOVEMBER 1998

Sunday,
NOVEMBER
1

Monday,
NOVEMBER
2

Tuesday,
NOVEMBER
3
Election Day (U.S.)

Wednesday,
NOVEMBER
4
Full Moon

Thursday,
NOVEMBER
5
Guy Fawkes Day (U.K.)

Friday,
NOVEMBER
6

Saturday,
NOVEMBER
7

NOVEMBER

S	M	T	W	T	F	S
1	2	3	4	5	6	7
8	9	10	11	12	13	14
15	16	17	18	19	20	21
22	23	24	25	26	27	28
29	30					

NOVEMBER 1998

Sunday,
NOVEMBER
8

Monday,
NOVEMBER
9

Tuesday,
NOVEMBER
10

Wednesday,
NOVEMBER
11
Veteran's Day
Remembrance Day (Canada)

Thursday,
NOVEMBER
12

Friday,
NOVEMBER
13

Saturday,
NOVEMBER
14

NOVEMBER

S	M	T	W	T	F	S
1	2	3	4	5	6	7
8	9	10	11	12	13	14
15	16	17	18	19	20	21
22	23	24	25	26	27	28
29	30					

NOVEMBER 1998

Sunday,
NOVEMBER
15

Monday,
NOVEMBER
16

Tuesday,
NOVEMBER
17

Wednesday,
NOVEMBER
18

Thursday,
NOVEMBER
19
New Moon

Friday,
NOVEMBER
20

Saturday,
NOVEMBER
21

NOVEMBER 1998

S	M	T	W	T	F	S
1	2	3	4	5	6	7
8	9	10	11	12	13	14
15	16	17	18	19	20	21
22	23	24	25	26	27	28
29	30					

Sunday,
NOVEMBER
22

Monday,
NOVEMBER
23

Tuesday,
NOVEMBER
24

Wednesday,
NOVEMBER
25

Thursday,
NOVEMBER
26

Thanksgiving Day (U.S.)

Friday,
NOVEMBER
27

Saturday,
NOVEMBER
28

NOVEMBER

S	M	T	W	T	F	S
1	2	3	4	5	6	7
8	9	10	11	12	13	14
15	16	17	18	19	20	21
22	23	24	25	26	27	28
29	30					

NOV. - DEC. 1998

Sunday,
NOVEMBER
29
Advent

Monday,
NOVEMBER
30

Tuesday,
DECEMBER
1

DECEMBER

S	M	T	W	T	F	S
		1	2	3	4	5
6	7	8	9	10	11	12
13	14	15	16	17	18	19
20	21	22	23	24	25	26
27	28	29	30	31		

Wednesday,
DECEMBER
2

Thursday,
DECEMBER
3
Full Moon

Friday,
DECEMBER
4

Saturday,
DECEMBER
5

DECEMBER 1998

DECEMBER

S	M	T	W	T	F	S
		1	2	3	4	5
6	7	8	9	10	11	12
13	14	15	16	17	18	19
20	21	22	23	24	25	26
27	28	29	30	31		

Sunday,
DECEMBER
6

Monday,
DECEMBER
7

Tuesday,
DECEMBER
8

Wednesday,
DECEMBER
9

Thursday,
DECEMBER
10

Friday,
DECEMBER
11

Saturday,
DECEMBER
12

DECEMBER

S M T W T F S
            1   2   3   4   5
6   7   8   9   10 11 12
13 14 15 16 17 18 19
20 21 22 23 24 25 26
27 28 29 30 31

DECEMBER 1998

Sunday,
DECEMBER
13

Monday,
DECEMBER
14
Hanukkah
(Feast of Dedication,
Festival of Lights)

Tuesday,
DECEMBER
15

Wednesday,
DECEMBER
16

Thursday,
DECEMBER
17

Friday,
DECEMBER
18
New Moon

Saturday,
DECEMBER
19

DECEMBER 1998

DECEMBER

S	M	T	W	T	F	S
		1	2	3	4	5
6	7	8	9	10	11	12
13	14	15	16	17	18	19
20	21	22	23	24	25	26
27	28	29	30	31		

Sunday,
DECEMBER
20

Monday,
DECEMBER
21

Tuesday,
DECEMBER
22
Winter Solstice

Wednesday,
DECEMBER
23

Thursday,
DECEMBER
24

Friday,
DECEMBER
25
Christmas Day

Saturday,
DECEMBER
26
Boxing Day (Canada, U.K.)

DECEMBER 1998

S	M	T	W	T	F	S
		1	2	3	4	5
6	7	8	9	10	11	12
13	14	15	16	17	18	19
20	21	22	23	24	25	26
27	28	29	30	31		

DEC. 1998 - JAN. 1999

Sunday,
DECEMBER
27

Monday,
DECEMBER
28

Tuesday,
DECEMBER
29

Wednesday,
DECEMBER
30

Thursday,
DECEMBER
31
New Year's Eve

Friday,
JANUARY
1
New Year's Day

JANUARY 1999

S	M	T	W	T	F	S
					1	2
3	4	5	6	7	8	9
10	11	12	13	14	15	16
17	18	19	20	21	22	23
24	25	26	27	28	29	30
31						

Saturday,
JANUARY
2